Book Of Poems

Hunt Family Book of Poems

Vera Hunt

India | USA | UK

Copyright © Vera Hunt
All Rights Reserved.

This book has been self-published with all reasonable efforts taken to make the material error-free by the author. No part of this book shall be used, reproduced in any manner whatsoever without written permission from the author, except in the case of brief quotations embodied in critical articles and reviews.

The Author of this book is solely responsible and liable for its content including but not limited to the views, representations, descriptions, statements, information, opinions, and references ["Content"]. The Content of this book shall not constitute or be construed or deemed to reflect the opinion or expression of the Publisher or Editor. Neither the Publisher nor Editor endorse or approve the Content of this book or guarantee the reliability, accuracy, or completeness of the Content published herein and do not make any representations or warranties of any kind, express or implied, including but not limited to the implied warranties of merchantability, fitness for a particular purpose.

The Publisher and Editor shall not be liable whatsoever...

Made with ❤ on the BookLeaf Publishing Platform
www.bookleafpub.in
www.bookleafpub.com

Dedication

For my Family who inspire me to try new adventures and keep me moving forward.

Preface

This collection of poems was written over the course of 30 years. They are my family's memories of younger days. I have formatted some with AI, but most are originals. I hope you enjoy them

Thank You
11/03/2025
Mid-Michigan
Vera Hunt

Acknowledgements

To my family:

My deepest gratitude goes to my family, who have been
my constant source of inspiration and strength
throughout this journey
Thank you for the beautiful; bond that we share, without
it I would be lost.

1. Harvest Moon in Barry County

Under the harvest moon, wide and gold,
The fields of wheat and soybeans fold
Into the hum of engines slow,
As farmers reap what summer sowed.

Cool air drifts through the colorful trees,
Bright reds, yellow, orange—a masterpiece.
The earth exhales in cool rains' grace,
And I see my breath in the morning's face.

Pumpkins rest in furrowed rows,

Round as moons the daylight knows.
The air turns breezy with autumn's scent—
Diesel, dust, and sunlight spent.

Hayrides rumble down the lane,
Children laughing, cheeks like flame.
Mugs of apple cider steam,
Sweet as a small-town harvest dream.

The days grow shorter, shadows run,
Yet I lift my face to the late-day sun,
Feeling its heat—a fleeting kiss,
Before the cold claims nights like this.

In Barry County, the season slows,
The land remembers all it grows.
Beneath that quiet, amber moon,
The world exhales—and rests—too soon.

-- Dr. Kevin H. Hunt

2. Rain

It was a nice night
The rain was just right.
It rained on the roof
It rained all night.

The rain came down with welcoming sounds
It came down on the gardens and down on the towns.
The rain kept coming with no end in sight
It flooded the gutters and took out the lights.

The trees lost leaves
And the flowers bowed down.
We unplugged the computers and TVs,
That didn't bug me.

We had cookies and milk under candle light
Until it was time to say good night.
The rain started to relax with a soft sleepy tap,
I was glad to hear that.

The rain went away and the night went calm.
The kids were asleep and the TV was back on.
I was sorry to have to say goodbye,
Until next time, may we all stay dry.

-- Vera Hunt

3. Tension

There's so much tension in our nation,
I believe I need a long vacation.

Politicians give ovations,
About our not so perfect nation.

We watch them on TV with fascination,
When we really should be helping our needy nation.

To do this you don't have to be a politician,
You could be a physician or musician.

Our condition is getting worse every day,
Why does it have to be this way?

But I'm in no position to say how the world works,
Though we all have a notion that it's getting worse.

Can't we all be happy for once?
Not to fight and get rid of guns.

Where are all the glorious days?
They won't be back unless we change our ways.

Let's come together, hand in hand,
Building a future where understanding stands.

-- Kevin A Hunt

4. The Indian's Hunting Song

Shawnee, Cherokee, Chickasaw,
I'm better than them all.
I track through whispering woods so near,
My arrows fly true, precise, and clear.

Shawnee, Cherokee, Chickasaw,
I'm better than them all.
With courage fierce and spirit bright,
I rise with the dawn, ready for the fight.

Shawnee, Cherokee, Chickasaw,
I'm better than them all!!!
In the heartbeat of the wild, I stand tall,
The legend of the Pawnee will never fall.

-- Tyler Hunt

5. My Day

I wake up in the mornings light.
The trees have such a huge height.
They seem to stretch and touch the sky,
They make me wish that I could fly.
I look over the hills and see the sun,
It reminds me the days just begun.
So, as I take in the smell of dew,
I hear the cry of a Robin's coo,
I take a bath in a cool spring,
As I listen to the Blue Bird's sing.
Soon the day begins to end,
And the colors of the next day blend.

-- Kevin A Hunt

6. Weather in Indiana

The weather changes all the time.
Some days the sun will shine.
Some days the clouds will snow,
and the ground will start to glow.
Some days it will rain and storm
And dark clouds start to form.
Some days the wind will blow,
All the leaves to-and-fro.
Some days fog creeps up in the night,
Right before the mornings light.
And that's the weather when you live in Indiana

-- Kevin A Hunt

7. Morning

The dog has been put out
And the kittens have been fed

That's a new job
That I don't even dread

The coffee done
And the showers began to run

Breakfast ready
I cook it just for fun

The Husbands on his way
And the kids have eaten, Yea

It is time for the bus
And the book bags are grabbed and they run off without fuss

The dog rides down to the bus stop

And one of the kids wants money for a pop

The buses have gone
And I'm alone

Me the kittens, the dog
And the phone.

It was a good morning
No one was snorting

It's mornings like this
That I can't call boring

I loved each and every monument
of this wonderful morning

I hope the rest of the day
is as calm in every way.

-- Vera Hunt

8. Silver Daisy

The Silver Daisy

It looks like a silver daisy bright,
Its petals gleam in morning light.
It stands so tall, with steadfast grace,
Watching o'er the neighborhood's face.

A stoic guard through calm or storm,
It braves the north wind, sharp and worn.
Yet smiles when southern breezes play,
Cool winds of summer light its day.

By moonlit hush, it still will turn,
Through night's deep hours, its heart will churn.
Ever present, firm and true,
A friend the sky forever knew.

Seen from miles, its blades still gleam,
A symbol born of work and dream.
In family hearts its memory stays,

The silver daisy of our days.

-- Dr. Kevin Hunt

9. Ebenezer

Ebenezer adds and subtracts all day,
He doesn't let anyone get in his way.

He loves to count and stay in the red,
If he sees black, you are dead.

Yeah, that old Eb measures right down to the inch,
He doesn't let anything slide by a pinch.

He is a miser of sorts,
Cutting old pants into shorts.

Ebenezer looks at your screen when he passes by,
Hoping to catch you, so he can stop and ask why?

He counts the coffee filters,
The coffee and tea,
When he's done, he always looks at me.

Eb keeps track of our trips to the coffee pot,

He's right on our heels with a little trot.

We can't wash the carpets until,
There are two more spots.

Leave that one to me,
I can do it by four.

Now don't get me wrong,
I like hearing Ebenezer's counting songs.

Without his counting, we would no longer be,
The counted company of Triple XYZ.

-- Vera Hunt

10. A Witches Love

*Is it the flowers or is it the sunset
Or is it just being with you that makes me forget,
Our past of so many years
Our future is not in the mirror.*

*I am happy and light,
High on nothing but life.
Smiling for no reason,
Enjoying the season.*

*I feel a sensation when we touch,
Like a cool breeze that I long for so much.
I want the day to slow down, this moment to stay.
I want to remember this day in every way.*

*I take a deep smell of the flowers,
A long look at the sun,
You leave in one hour, and my emotions have started to run.*

You have changed your mind?
You're not going away?
Will! I haven't changed mine!
I was going to the mall.

It was nice to see you, but I haven't changed my mind to leave
I can't sit here all night under this tree
Yes, I know what I said, and I know you changed your mind for me.
But I wasn't expecting you to get down on one knee.

Please forgive me for running,
I want what I can't have.
If only you left and let me be sad.
It was all I expected.
Please don't be mad.

But still, as the dusk paints the sky in gold,
There's a warmth in your smile, a story untold.
Could it be that the flowers and sunset collide,
In the space where our hearts, unexpectedly, bide?

So, let's linger a moment, let worries dissolve,
In the beauty around us, let our hearts evolve.
For what if this moment, like petals, might bloom,

Could it blossom in twilight, dispel all the gloom?
-- Vera Hunt

11. Remember Me

I'm not done with life yet.
I hope you haven't placed your bet.
I try and try to complete my task,
But my list of jobs gets longer very fast.

I only want to leave a little treat,
To everyone I meet.
To help you remember me,
I'm the one that drinks catnip tea.

I'm the one who you call when you're sad,
I always have a new way to make you glad.
I have a smile in my pocket just waiting for you.
All you have to do, is cry Boo! Hoo!

I like being your happy piece,
It makes me feel like I'm your favorite niece.
I'm not a good luck charm,
But I'm needed just the same.
I like seeing you smile; it's not at all lame.

I'm not done with life yet,
I need to leave a little more.
Maybe a painting, maybe a book.
I know both will have a special kind of look.

I may even try my hand in a different kind of garden.
It will have a velvet moss floor,
With the kinds of plants that spread and make more.
I can share with friends galore.

It must have a pond with a fountain,
And lots of tiny lights.
Sitting in it will make you calm,
You'll want to sit in it all night.

I do these things to leave for you,
A place to sit and cry Boo Hoo
There's nothing better than a space to recharge,
Where laughter lingers and memories enlarge.

It's a sanctuary for your weary heart,
A canvas where our stories can start.
A whisper in the breeze, a chuckle in the sun,
With every moment shared, our spirits become one.

So, when the shadows begin to play,

And the world feels heavy at the end of the day,
Remember me fondly, just look around,
In the laughter and love, my essence is found.

I'm not done with life yet; hear my song,
In every heartbeat, where you belong.
I'm not dead yet, but I can hear you just the same,
Together, we'll dance in the light, play this beautiful game.

-- Vera Hunt

12. Barbara

I thought I'd take the time to say,
I like you in so many ways.

I love your happy, go-lucky smile,
I wish we had more time to chat awhile.

I value your opinions and always want to hear it,
Good bad or indifferent I never fear it.

I like the way you organize,
you know where everything is, better than the guys.

I love when you play your guitar, what a sweet surprise
I hope the children remember it, when looking into the past.

we need more people like you,
who will share their point of view.

I've enjoyed this school year and how you've helped me

grow,
I respect you and your family more than you know.

-- Vera Hunt

13. Missing You

I feel so lazy, I can't get up.
I yawn and yawn into my coffee cup.

I've had six cups, I should have one more,
But I'm so tired, I don't think I could walk across the floor.

If only I could get a jumpstart,
I'd possibly be able to play my part.

Please, please, I say,
Don't just stay parked where you lie.

Get up, get up,
enjoy the day,

But here I sit, coffee in hand,
Waiting for inspiration to expand

It hasn't come, and my coffee is cold,

It's making my teeth taste like mold.

Wait! I feel it coming on.
I'm walking, now, running!
Imagine that.

If only you were here,
I wouldn't have to go through this.

Missing you
makes everything a miss.

-- Vera Hunt

14. Halloween with Ryan

Halloween with Ryan

Pumpkins glowing orange bright,
Flicker softly through the night.
Ryan smiles, her eyes so wide,
As candy buckets fill with pride.

Down the street the houses gleam,
Each one looks like a spooky dream!
Ghosts that giggle, witches fly,
Bats and cobwebs drift on by.

Hand in hand with Mommy dear,
Daddy laughs and gives a cheer.
Grandpa joins the happy crew,
Telling jokes as grandpas do!

They ring the bells at every door,
Candy, chocolate — more and more!
Ryan dances, full of glee,
Best Halloween there'll ever be.

But as the moon climbs high above,
Grandpa waves with so much love.
Ryan hugs him, soft and slow —
"Come back soon, don't ever go!"

Stars are twinkling, pumpkins shine,
What a night — sweet Halloween time!
Dreams of candy fill her head,
As Ryan snuggles into bed

-- Dr. Kevin Hunt

15. Arcola School

Arcola school is full of people,
and has many stars, too.
If you want to see someone special,
you don't have to look too far.

Arcola school is a beautiful place,
in the county with lots of trees.
Be careful when you run outside-
you may also see some bees.

Arcola has bright colors,
the school is lots of fun.
The play ground is full of kids,
with lots of room to run.

Arcola school has nice rooms and teachers,
and a library full of books.
When I tell people I wish I went all year long,
they give me funny looks.

It is time for Arcola to shut its doors,
but, I'll be back next year.
I hope to learn much, much more,
and see my friends so dear.

-- Tyler Hunt

16. Whales

When we study the big subject of whales,
we get out our paper and pencils
our glue and crayons
our hammer, nails, and pails.

We watch movies and read books
looking them up on the internet
with amazing awing looks.

We study their weight
their eating habits
and their homes

We study the kinds of whales
the length they are
and their bones.

And why you ask
do we study something so faraway
so large that to see it

would make us afraid.

In the hopes that one of our children
just one,
will go on to save the whales.

Whales for our future,
and whales for our children's future.
not to mention the fun.

-- Kevin A. Hunt

17. The Snow Falls

As the snow falls to the ground,
My confidence will rise, unbound.
As the cold winter winds blow,
My creative abilities will grow.

As the bulbs in spring begin to sprout,
My adventures in my life roll out.
As the heat of summer flames,
My smiles fill with unexplored miles.

As the Yule log burns bright,
My future churns in the night.
As the problems of last year go up in smoke,
My last year's curses are broken and revoked.

As the future events align themselves.
My outcome that pleases me devolves
As the new year opens wide,
My love for life turns to gold.

Open the upper realms of the skies,
Open the gates where the underworld lies.
Let the vision of the living and the dead,
Speak to me within my head.

-- Vera Hunt

18. Sing, Ring, and Dance

As I sing and ring by bells,
I am noticed and assisted by havens realm.
As I sing and ring my bells,
I am filled with positive thought and gifts offered by a witch elm.

As I pray and sprinkle my salt,
I am proio9tected and blessed as I chalk.
As I pray and sprinkle my salt'
I am surrounded by angles of light as I walk.

As I light my candles of elements,
I am assisted by water, fire, earth, and air.
ASs I light my candles of elements,
I am empowered by the element energy everywhere.

As I dance and smudge my home,
I am accompanied by positive unknowns.
As I dance and smudge my home,
I am filled with positive energy as if it was in blown,

With assistance from Haven and Me.

So-Be-It!
-- Vera Hunt

19. Negative out Positive In

As the negative energy leaves my home,
Positive, calmness and protection enter alone.
As the negative energy leaves my home,
Problems of the past dissipate and leave me alone
As the negative energy leaves by home,
Positive energy of health, wealth, and love are grown.

-- Vera Hunt

20. Grandma's Sugar Cake

I was visiting Grandma one summer date...
When she decided we should whip up a cake.

Grandma was excited as she jumped to a start...
she grabbed all the tools required for her art.

She pulled out wooden tools, rubber spatulas and spoons...
so many things so quickly I started to swoon.

She pulled out pans of several sizes and shapes...
with removable bottoms and sides ... All this for cake?

We cut wax paper circles for pan bottoms and tops...
and squares for the counter when the cakes come out hot.

We sprinkled flour on our hands, pans, counter and more...

a little even ended up on the floor.

We got out that giant countertop mixer...
with proper bowls and beaters to mix our elixir.

We got out double boilers, filled with water just so...
separated yokes from the whites which we cooked very slow.

We added the ingredients in the proper order to ensure...
our frosting would not "sugar" or fail and not cure.

We mixed, we kneaded, we stirred, and we whipped...
we laughed; we giggled and snickered a bit.

We poked it with toothpicks and with knives, forks, and spoons...
to ensure it was not removed from the oven too soon.

We slathered on frosting as we stacked up the cake...
and used dowel rod and toothpick to ensure our cakes state.

We tasted with fingers and forks by the liters ...
(read quietly) and I not-so-secretly licked off the beaters.

When we were done, we sat and enjoyed that silky cake

...

which Grandpa ate with enjoyment I'm sure was not fake.

No cake as ever tasted better, or more fun to make...
Main ingredients of fun, and love's all it takes.

-- Tyler Hunt

www.ingramcontent.com/pod-product-compliance
Lightning Source LLC
Chambersburg PA
CBHW070040070426
42449CB00012BA/3115